GO FOR IT!

GO FOR IT!

a photographic celebration

morrow

I like it, I do it. That's my code.

Alan Denlon

Be not afraid of going

slowly, be only afraid of

standing still.

Chinese Proverb

Do something.

Either lead, follow, or get out of the way.

Ted Turner

They say you can't do it, but remember,

that doesn't always work.

Casey Stengel

The aim of living is life itself.

Johann Wolfgang von Goethe

Ever tried. Ever failed. No matter.

Try again. Fail again. Fail better.

Samuel Beckett

There is no such thing as great talent

without great will-power.

Honoré de Balzac

Per ardua ad astra

(by striving we reach the stars)

Royal Air Force motto

It is easier to begin well than to finish well.

Plautus

Have a go. Anybody can do it.

Alan Parker

It's not a successful climb

unless you enjoy the journey.

Dan Benson

Never discourage anyone…who continually makes

progress, no matter how slow.

Plato

Courage is its own reward.

Plautus

Life is a succession of moments.

To live each one is to succeed.

Corita Kent

Eighty percent of success is

showing up.

Woody Allen

If at first you don't succeed,

you're doing about average.

Leonard Louis Levinson

Whatever doesn't kill you,

makes you stronger.

Marlon Brando

If it isn't happening, *make* it happen.

David Hemmings

Nothing great was ever

achieved without enthusiasm.

Ralph Waldo Emerson

The world is always

ready to receive talent

with open arms.

Oliver Wendell Holmes

All that I can, I will.

French Saying

There is no penalty for overachievement.

George William Miller

Bravery is believing in yourself, and that thing nobody can teach you.

El Cordobés

The only people who never fail

are those who never try.

Ilka Chase

Great works are

performed not

by strength

but by

perseverance.

Samuel Johnson

Many would be cowards

if they had courage enough.

Proverb

Activity is contagious.

Ralph Waldo Emerson

Act as if it were impossible to fail.

Dorothea Brande

Man needs difficulties; they are necessary for health.

Carl Jung

The road to success is always under construction.

Arnold Palmer

As long as you're

going to think anyway,

think big.

Donald Trump

With enough courage,

you can do without a reputation.

Clarke Gable

Man's aspiration is absurd;

it is by what he discovers that he is great.

Paul Valéry

No one knows what is in him till he

tries, and many would never try if they

were not forced to.

Basil W. Maturin

Just keep going.

Everybody gets better if they keep at it.

Ted Williams

You see things; and you say, "Why?"

But I dream things that never were;

and I say, "Why not?"

George Bernard Shaw

There's never any talent

without a little stain of madness.

Jean-Louis Trintignant

Winning is living.

Every time you win, you're reborn.

George Allen

To see one's goal and to drive toward it,

steeling one's heart, is most uplifting.

Henrik Ibsen

Success is never final and failure never fatal.

It's courage that counts.

George Tilton

Don't look back.

Something may be gaining on you.

Satchel Paigne

Sweat is the cologne of accomplishment.

Heywood Hale Brown

When you reach the top, that's when the climb begins.

Michael Caine

We strain hardest for things which are almost

but not quite within our reach.

Frederick W. Faber

Success and failure are both greatly overrated.

But failure gives you a whole lot more to talk about.

Hildegard Knef

The only place where success comes

before work is in a dictionary.

Vidal Sassoon

Success covers many blunders.

George Bernard Shaw

It ain't over 'til it's over.

Yogi Berra

Effort is only effort when it begins to hurt.

José Ortega y Gasset

Nature gave man two ends – one to sit

on and one to think with. Ever since,

man's success has been dependent on

the one he uses most.

George R. Fitzpatrick

Overcome the earth, and the stars shall be yours.

Boethius

Learn as if you were to live forever;

live as if you were to die tomorrow.

Anonymous

Just go out there and do what you've got to do.

Anonymous

Picture Credits

cover: Triple jump, 1964.

title page: A rodeo rider is thrown by a bucking horse, circa 1960.

page 4/5: Holiday makers enjoying the chair-o-plane ride at a fairground in Epsom, Surrey, UK, 1950.

page 6/7: The Taylor quads on their pogo sticks, London, UK, 1958.

page 8: Robinson cycling park, France, 1955.

page 11: Lifeguards in a balancing contest, Sydney, Australia, 1931.

page 12/13: A group of girls, Sydney, Australia, 1931.

page 14/15: As title page.

page 17: Practicing high-wire cycling in the back garden, 1939.

page 19: The Marquis Trio performing on the beach near Dymchurch, Kent, UK, 1946.

page 20: Eddie Kidd in mid-flight, Essex, UK, 1979.

page 22: Women on the beach at Hastings, UK, 1938.

page 25: Children playing on a commando-style training net, Fulham, London, UK, 1952.

page 26: Leapfrog in a street, London, UK, 1950.

page 28: Oxford University's swimming team preparing for the day's practice, 1936.

page 31: The water chute ride at Battersea Pleasure Gardens, London, UK, 1964.

page 32/33: A rocking horse Derby, Royal Botanic Gardens, London, UK, 1926.

page 34: Two women roller-skating, Hastings, UK, 1934.

page 36/37: The "greasy pole", Sark Regatta, 1925.

page 38: Football practice, Scarsdale, New York, US, circa 1954.

page 40/41: Clark's shoes being given a rigorous test by children in Somerset, UK, 1955.

page 42/43: A water-skiing waiter, Woerthersee Lake, Kaemten, Austria, 1969.

page 45: A trapeze artist from Chapman's high-wire team, circa 1950.

page 47: Water skiing at Cypress Gardens, Florida, US, 1965. Band Photos/Hulton Getty Picture Collection.

page 48/49: A stuntman in a customised plane, Alexandra Palace, London, UK, 1930.

page 51: Water ski champion, Dick Pope, at the center of a human pyramid, Cypress Gardens, Florida, US, 1965. Band Photos/Hulton Getty Picture Collection

page 52/53: 15-month-old Franziska Dressler walks a tightrope, 1950.

page 54/55: A little boy hides during the climax of a trapeze act, circa 1955.

Copyright © 2000 M Q Publications Limited

All rights reserved. No part of this book may be reproduced or utilized in any form or by
any means, electronic or mechanical, including photocopying, recording, or by any
information storage or retrieval system, without permission in writing from the Publisher.
Inquiries should be addressed to Permissions Department, William Morrow and
Company, Inc., 1350 Avenue of the Americas, New York, N.Y. 10019.

It is the policy of William Morrow and Company, Inc., and its imprints and affiliates,
recognizing the importance of preserving what has been written, to print the books we
publish on acid-free paper, and we exert our best efforts to that end.

ISBN: 0-688-17701-8

Library of Congress Cataloging-in-Publication Data

CIP data has been applied for.

Printed in China
First Edition
2 3 4 5 6 7 8 9 10

Cover design: John Casey
Design: WDA
Text and picture research: Suzie Green
Series Editor: Elizabeth Carr